Snap books™

Crafts

Valentines

Cards and Crafts from the Heart

by Thiranut Boonyadhistarn

Capstone press®

Mankato, Minnesota

Snap Books are published by Capstone Press,
151 Good Counsel Drive, P.O. Box 669, Mankato, Minnesota 56002.
www.capstonepress.com

Library of Congress Cataloging-in-Publication Data
Boonyadhistarn, Thiranut.
  Valentines : cards and crafts from the heart / by Thiranut
Boonyadhistarn.
    p. cm.—(Snap books. Crafts)
    Summary: "A do-it-yourself crafts book for children and pre-teens
on making valentines"—Provided by publisher.
    Includes bibliographical references and index.
    ISBN-13: 978-0-7368-6475-6 (hardcover)
    ISBN-10: 0-7368-6475-X (hardcover)
    1. Valentine decorations—Juvenile literature. 2. Valentines—
Juvenile literature. 3. Handicraft—Juvenile literature. I. Title. II. Series.
TT900.V34B66 2007
745.594'1618—dc22   2006004079

Editor: Megan Schoeneberger
Designer: Bobbi J. Wyss
Production Artist: Renée T. Doyle
Photo Researcher: Kelly Garvin

Photo Credits:
All photos by Capstone Press/Karon Dubke, except page 32 by Aubrey Whitten

1 2 3 4 5 6 11 10 09 08 07 06

Go Metric!

It's easy to change measurements to metric! Just use this chart.

To change	into	multiply by
inches	centimeters	2.54
inches	millimeters	25.4
feet	meters	.305
yards	meters	.914
ounces (liquid)	milliliters	29.57
ounces (liquid)	liters	.029
cups (liquid)	liters	.237
pints	liters	.473
quarts	liters	.946
gallons	liters	3.78
ounces (dry)	grams	28.35
pounds	grams	453.59

Table of Contents

CHAPTER 1

Hooray for Valentine's Day

It's not just for sweethearts anymore.

We all think Valentine's Day is just for girlfriends and boyfriends, husbands and wives—a bunch of mushy stuff for people in love. Think again. Valentine's Day is not really about people *in* love. It's more about the people *you* love. So that means more than just your boyfriends and crushes. That means your best friends, your grandparents, your mom and dad, even your little brother.

On Valentine's Day, people usually give the same type of gifts, like pre-boxed chocolates and store-bought cards. But you can put a new spin on Valentine's Day. With the projects in this book, your family and friends (and even your crushes) will know your valentines really came from the heart. Just turn the page and let the fun begin!

CHAPTER 2

My Fuzzy Valentine

Who doesn't love fun fur?

Give your friends and family a real warm fuzzy with this valentine. These furry hearts will show how soft-hearted you can be.

Here's what you need

* ✳ pink or red poster board
* ✳ scissors
* ✳ pencil and eraser
* ✳ markers
* ✳ pink or red **fun fur**
* ✳ craft glue
* ✳ glitter, **rhinestones**, confetti, and other decorations

Here's what you do

1 Cut out a 6-inch by 6-inch square section of poster board.

2 Draw a heart on the square section of poster board, filling in as much of the space as possible.

3 Lightly write a valentine message in pencil on the heart. Go over your message in markers. Do not cut the heart out yet.

4 Cut out a 6-inch by 6-inch section of fun fur.

5 Glue the poster board to the back of the fun fur. Make sure the side with the Valentine's Day message is facing out. Let it dry for 60 to 90 minutes.

6 After the glue has dried, cut out the heart shape and erase any stray pencil marks.

7 Decorate your heart with glitter, confetti, and rhinestones, then give it to someone you really like or love.

7

CHAPTER 3

Message in a Bottle

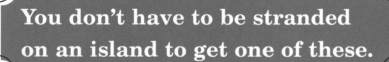

You don't have to be stranded on an island to get one of these.

Looking for a new way to recycle used bottles? Here's the best one yet. Your friends will love the mystery as they unroll the note to see what you've written inside. So start collecting those bottles, and send your friends a valentine they'll treasure.

The best bottles for this project should be clear with a long neck. But make sure the opening isn't too small. Remember you need to be able to fit the message through the opening, so hot sauce bottles may not be such a good idea. Check craft stores for miniature glass bottles if you want to make lots of these to give to all your friends.

Here's what you need

* clean, clear, small- to medium-sized glass or plastic bottles
* pencil and eraser
* pink, red, or lavender poster board
* scissors
* markers
* glitter, rhinestones, confetti, and other decorations
* craft glue
* hot glue gun and glue stick
* pink, red, or lavender pipe cleaners
* pink, red, or lavender writing paper
* pourable, colorful candy, such as cinnamon red hots, jelly beans, or candy sprinkles
* pink or red felt
* pink or red ribbon or yarn
* **wire cutter**

Here's what you do

1 Draw and cut out a heart from the poster board, about ¼ the height of the bottle. Erase any stray pencil marks.

2 Decorate the heart however you like.

3 Hot glue a pipe cleaner to the back of the heart, then set it aside.

4 Cut out a square of writing paper about ⅔ the height of the bottle.

5 Write your valentine message on the paper, starting out with pencil and then going over it with markers. Set the message aside.

6 Fill the bottle ⅔ of the way with candy.

7 Roll up the valentine message and put it into the mouth of the bottle until the bottom of the message reaches into the candy. Then let the message unroll a bit to secure itself in the mouth of the bottle.

8 Cut a piece of felt just wide and long enough to go around the opening of the bottle.

9 Dab glue around the opening of the bottle, then glue the felt around it. This way you'll cover up the ridges at the top of the bottle.

10 Tie ribbon or yarn around the opening of the bottle.

11 Wrap the pipe cleaner with the heart on it around the middle of the bottle. Twist the pipe cleaner to secure it, then cut off the extra with wire cutters.

CHAPTER 4

Bouquet of Hearts

Bring a whole new meaning to the term "sweethearts."

Pile on the sweetness with this unique cookie bouquet. It may be a lot of work to put together, but it will be worth it. Your valentines will eat their hearts out when they see what you've cooked up for them.

Here's what you need

* flowerpot
* tube of refrigerated sugar cookie dough
* rolling pin
* heart-shaped cookie cutter
* nonstick cookie sheet
* lollipop sticks or wooden skewers
* frosting and candy cookie decorations in Valentine's Day colors
* Styrofoam cut to fit inside flowerpot
* candies such as conversation hearts to cover the Styrofoam in the flowerpot

Here's what you do

1 Roll out the cookie dough to about ⅛-inch thick. Use the cookie cutter to cut out heart shapes.

2 Insert a lollipop stick or a wooden skewer into each cookie before baking.

3 Bake the cookies according to package instructions and let them cool.

4 Frost and decorate the cookies. Let the cookies sit uncovered overnight so the frosting can harden.

5 Place the Styrofoam into the flowerpot.

6 Stick the cookies into the Styrofoam. Add a layer of candy to hide the Styrofoam, and your bouquet is ready.

CHAPTER 5

A Fortune in Valentines

You will take an exciting trip!

What's the best part of ordering Chinese food? The cookie, of course.

Put a new twist on the classic fortune cookie and turn it into a one-of-a-kind valentine. Dress it up with pink frosting and cake decorations. Then write your own message. You'll have a fortune in Valentine's Day pals after giving out these sweet treats.

Only in America
You might think fortune cookies come from China. But they don't. They're mostly given out in Chinese restaurants in the United States and Canada. Restaurants in China call them "genuine American fortune cookies."

Here's what you need

* white paper
* scissors
* pen or marker
* poster board
* pencil and eraser
* hot glue gun and glue stick
* toothpicks
* fortune cookies
* frosting
* candy sprinkles and colored sugar

Turn the page to get started.

15

Here's what you do

1 Cut strips of white paper ½ inch by 2 inches.

2 Write your valentine fortunes on the strips with pen or marker. Set them aside.

3 Draw hearts about 2 inches wide on the poster board. You'll need two hearts for each cookie.

4 Cut them out and erase any stray pencil marks. Add decorations to the hearts as desired.

5 Glue two hearts together along the sides, leaving the top open like a pocket, with a toothpick in the bottom.

6 Tuck a valentine fortune into each heart-shaped pocket.

7 Working on one fortune cookie at a time, cover the cookie with frosting. Sprinkle candy sprinkles or colored sugar over the frosted cookie.

8 Stick a heart on a toothpick in the center fold of the cookie.

9 Let your friends choose their fortune cookies and discover what their futures hold.

A Fortune Forever

These frosted fortunes won't last long before they're gobbled up. To make them more permanent, try this version. Paint the fortune cookies with **acrylic paints** or cover them in glitter. Attach everything with hot glue instead of frosting. Your pals won't be able to eat these, but they can keep them forever.

CHAPTER 6

My Heart's on a Chain

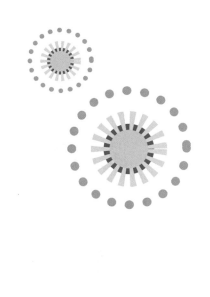

Even though these valentines are baked, they're not for snacking!

Cards, candies, and cookies are all great tokens of affection for Valentine's Day. But how about giving your gal pals something that'll remind them of you throughout the year? With the magic of **shrink plastic**, you can give out valentines that are also jewelry. You're sure to be everyone's favorite valentine with an idea like that.

Here's what you need

* sanding sponge (fine grain)
* clear shrink plastic
* colored pencils
* colored permanent markers
* scissors
* ¹⁄₁₆-inch hole punch
* cookie sheet
* **parchment paper**
* spatula
* **flat-nose pliers**
* 6- or 8-millimeter **jump rings**
* thin red or pink ribbon

Plan Ahead

Shrink plastic will shrink to about ¹⁄₂ to ¹⁄₃ its original size. It's a good idea to experiment a little to figure out what size to start with to get the finished size you want.

Here's what you do

1 Use the sanding sponge to sand a sheet of shrink plastic. If you skip this step, the colored pencils won't work on the shrink plastic.

2 Use colored pencils to draw and color some hearts about 2 inches wide. Lighter colors work best because they will darken during the baking process.

3 Write messages on the hearts with the permanent markers.

4 Cut out the hearts.

5 Punch one hole in the heart where the jump ring will go.

6 Cover the cookie sheet with parchment paper. Lay the hearts colored-side up on the sheet. Place a second sheet of parchment paper on top to keep the plastic from sticking to itself if it curls up during baking.

7 Bake the hearts according to the package instructions.

8 When the time is up, remove the cookie sheet from the oven. If any of the hearts are a bit curled up, flatten them with a spatula over the parchment paper while the plastic is still hot. Then wait at least 30 minutes for the hearts to cool and harden.

9 Use the flat-nose pliers to open and attach a jump ring to the holes in the hearts. Then close the jump ring.

10 Cut the ribbon to the length you want and thread it through the jump ring.

REMEMBER!

Safety Tip

Stay near the oven when you're baking shrink plastic. It usually takes only a few minutes.

CHAPTER 7

Munch to the Message

Everyone loves to get boxes of sweet treats for Valentine's Day.

But what happens after the munchies are all gone? All you have left is an empty box. Not with this treasure trove of treats. When your valentine gets to the last bite, she'll find your colorful message waiting at the bottom.

Here's what you need

* heart-shaped craft box
* fine-point permanent marker
* clear plastic protector sheet (glossy)
* scissors
* red or pink poster board
* pencil
* colorful sticky-backed letters or alphabet stickers
* acrylic craft paints
* decorations for your box
* craft glue
* treats to fill the box

Here's what you do

1 With the permanent marker, trace around the bottom of the heart box onto the plastic protector sheet.

2 Cut the heart out from the sheet. Place it inside the box to make sure it fits into the bottom. Keep cutting around the edges of the heart until it fits.

3 Repeat steps 1 through 3 to cut a heart from the poster board, except use a pencil in place of the permanent marker.

4 Use sticky letters for your valentine message on the heart. To be safe, don't use markers in case the ink runs onto the candy.

5 Paint and decorate the box.

6 Place the heart message in the bottom of the box, then put the plastic heart on top of it to protect it.

7 Fill the box with a sweet snack like caramel corn, chocolate kisses, gummies, or conversation hearts.

8 Put the lid on the box, and give it to a friend for Valentine's Day.

CHAPTER 8

A Display of Affection

Sometimes cards and candy just aren't enough.

Your best friend, boyfriend, mom, closest sibling, or favorite aunt—these loved ones are too near and dear for just chocolates and a card. Wouldn't you rather give them something truly precious to let them know how much you love them? A **shadow box** will show your loved ones how much you treasure having them in your life.

Boxes Undercover

To find the perfect box, you may want to start with your closet. A shoebox will make a great shadow box. Just cut down the sides so they are only a few inches deep. Then use spray paint, old wallpaper, or even gift wrap to disguise its true identity.

Here's what you need

- wooden shadow box or homemade shadow box
- acrylic paint
- hot glue gun and glue stick
- 1-inch square wooden or Styrofoam block
- scissors
- sticky letters or alphabet stickers
- craft glue
- glitter, rhinestones, pom-poms, and other decorations
- feather boa
- any other decorative item your valentine would like

Here's what you do

1 Paint the inside panel of the box red and the rest of the box pink. Painting the inside panel a darker color will give the illusion of the box being deeper.

2 Allow 60 to 90 minutes for the paint to dry.

3 Glue the small block in the middle of the inside panel.

4 Choose a centerpiece photo for the box, and cut it out in a heart shape. Set it aside.

5 Use the sticky letters to write your Valentine's Day message.

6 Decorate the inside of the panel of the box with glitter, pom-poms, and rhinestones.

7 Glue sections of the feather boa around the front edges of the box to cover any nails or staples that were used when the box was made.

8 Glue other items to the outside of the box that your valentine will like. They can be anything from little toys to vacation souvenirs to ticket stubs. But don't add so many things that the box is too busy. The photo should be the main feature of the box.

9 Glue the heart-shaped photo onto the wooden or Styrofoam block, and deliver your box to your valentine with lots of love.

Fast Facts

Valentine's Greetings Galore

According to the Greeting Card Association, about a billion Valentine's Day cards are sent out every year all over the world. So, who's buying those billion Valentines? Women buy about 85 percent of all of them!

Sweets for Sweeties

Candy store owners love Valentine's Day. That's because more boxes of chocolate sell on Valentine's Day than on any other day of the year. Each year, Americans purchase more than 36 million heart-shaped boxes of chocolate.

For the Birds

In the late 1300s, British poet Geoffrey Chaucer wrote that Valentine's Day was the day that birds flew off to find their mates. From that point on, Valentine's Day became associated with love. Before that, it was seen as just another feast day.

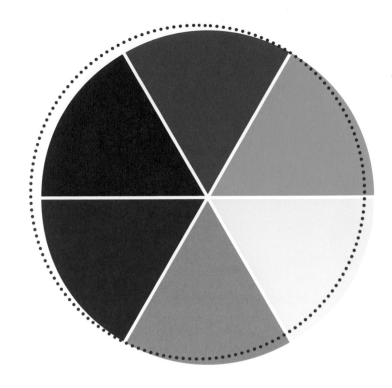

Color Wheel

Reds and pinks are popular for Valentine's Day. If you want to try some other colors in your projects, think about the color wheel. It shows how colors work with each other. The colors next to red work together in harmony, which might be good for valentines. Colors across from red have more contrast and a stronger effect.

Glossary

acrylic paint (uh-KRIL-ik PAYNT)—a type of paint made from chemicals and often used for crafts

flat-nose pliers (FLAT-NOHZ PLYE-urz)—a tool used in jewelry making to open and close jump rings and hold small pieces

fun fur (FUN FUR)—fake fur in bright colors used in crafts

jump ring (JUHMP RING)—small rings used to attach links and clasps in pieces of jewelry

parchment paper (PARCH-muhnt PAY-pur)—paper sold in rolls used for baking

rhinestone (RINE-stone)—a plastic jewel used in crafts and jewelry making

shadow box (SHAD-oh BOKS)—a shallow case in which something is set for display

shrink plastic (SHRINGK PLASS-tik)—a type of plastic found at most craft stores that shrinks when exposed to high temperatures

wire cutter (WIRE KUHT-uhr)—a tool used to cut craft and jewelry wire or chain

Read More

Corba, Anna. *Making Memory Boxes: 35 Beautiful Projects.* New York: Sterling, 2005.

Erlbach, Arlene, and Herb Erlbach. *Valentine's Day Crafts.* Fun Holiday Crafts Kids Can Do. Berkeley Heights, N.J.: Enslow, 2004.

Hitron, Noga, and Natasha Haimovich. *The Art of Cookies: Fast and Fun Cookie Decoration.* Berkeley, California: Ten Speed Press, 2004.

Internet Sites

FactHound offers a safe, fun way to find Internet sites related to this book. All of the sites on FactHound have been researched by our staff.

Here's how:

1. Visit *www.facthound.com*
2. Choose your grade level.
3. Type in this book ID **073686475X** for age-appropriate sites. You may also browse subjects by clicking on letters, or by clicking on pictures and words.
4. Click on the **Fetch It** button.

FactHound will fetch the best sites for you!

About the Author

Thiranut Boonyadhistarn grew up in Tokyo, Bangkok, and Chicago. She learned various crafts in each country: origami in Japan, beading in Thailand, and paper crafts in America. The crafts she learned as a child have led to a lifelong love of the arts.

Boonyadhistarn has worked in film and TV production, graphic design, and book production. She also has written several kids' books on crafts. She lives in a tiny apartment in New York City, surrounded by boxes of glitter, rhinestones, and craft glue.

Index